With best wishes from the
author

29.06.2003

THE BEST OF
LEICESTER

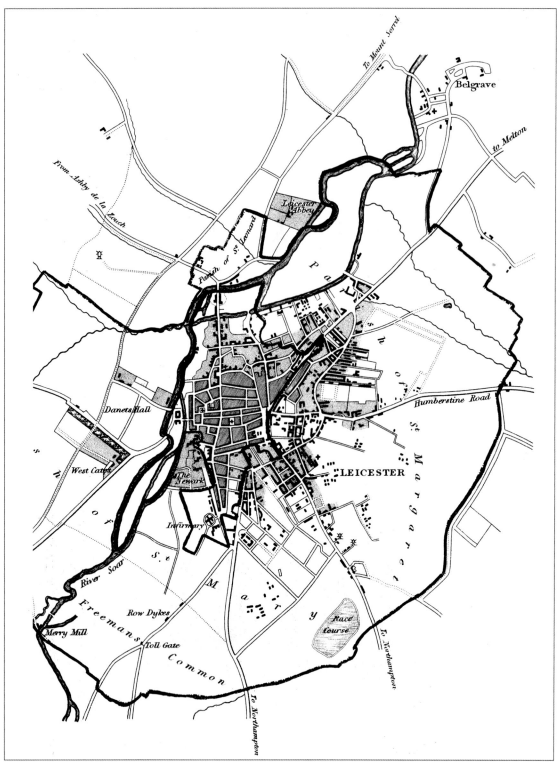

A map of the Borough of Leicester, drawn by R. Creighton and engraved and published by J. & C. Walker in 1835. Leicester was a small town built on the banks of the River Soar, surrounded by fields. Evidence on this map shows that a plan had been made for the start of the expansion of the Victorian town.

THE BEST OF
LEICESTER

T REVOR H ICKMAN

Semper Eadem – 'Always the Same'

SUTTON PUBLISHING

Sutton Publishing Limited
Phoenix Mill · Thrupp · Stroud
Gloucestershire · GL5 2BU

First published 2002

Copyright © Trevor Hickman, 2002

Title page: Gardens and castle, *c.* 1930.

British Library Cataloguing in Publication Data
A catalogue record for this book is available from the British Library.

ISBN 0-7509-3042-X

Typeset in 10.5/13.5 Photina.
Typesetting and origination by
Sutton Publishing Limited.
Printed and bound in England by
J.H. Haynes & Co. Ltd, Sparkford.

By the same author:

Around Melton Mowbray in Old Photographs
Melton Mowbray in Old Photographs
East of Leicester in Old Photographs
The Melton Mowbray Album
The Vale of Belvoir in Old Photographs
The History of the Melton Mowbray Pork Pie
The History of Stilton Cheese
Melton Mowbray to Oakham
Around Rutland in Old Photographs
Leicestershire Memories
The Best of East Leicestershire and Rutland

CONTENTS

London Road leading towards and passing through the parish of St Margaret in the first half of the eighteenth century. This is a section of the famous print *The South Prospect of Leicester*; in the centre stands the magnificent church of St Margaret. On the edge of the engraving to the right stands Leicester Abbey. This illustration is taken in part from the *Antiquities in England and Wales*, published as three volumes in 1774 by Samuel and Nathaniel Buck, in which there are 511 plates, 83 of which are double-page, folded spreads. These oblong folios are one of the finest series of copperplate engraved views of town and cities ever published, drawn on site by the Bucks, later to be engraved and printed in their workshop. During the nineteenth century most of these books were broken up and marketed as individual plates, at fairly high prices. This is part of plate no. 37, one of the double-page spreads, produced in March 1743. The volumes took over thirty years to complete!

INTRODUCTION

In my recent book *The Best of East Leicestershire & Rutland* I made some remarks about how to use the itinerary: by following the text and illustrations in the order presented. The reader should have allowed at least three whole days to search out those areas that I considered worth visiting. *The Best of Leicester* is the second book in my series 'The Best of', and again the reader is recommended to follow the very loose itinerary; the choice is the reader's. Anyone living in Leicester who follows the book, searching out the past and the present detailed in the following pages, will undoubtedly have their own ideas, especially concerning my comments, and will make up their own minds about what is worth seeing. Visitors to the city by car, bus and train can discover Leicester on foot, following the route suggested here. I recommend a walk along parts of the towpath of the Grand Union Canal that runs through the city, occasionally diverting to the footpaths that run along the banks of the River Soar, using the information that is available in this book.

If a more detailed itinerary is required visit the excellent Tourist Information Centre opposite the Town Hall. It holds an extremely useful collection of leaflets and flyers that will complement this book.

I compiled this book by walking around the ancient city with a good friend of many years, Don Humberston, Don has lived in the Belgrave area for over sixty years. In those years he has seen many of the changes that are described here. The two of us spent many hours walking through the city using footpaths and roads. We studied the map published in 1828 and (printed in part on page 112), and compared it with the current Ordnance Survey and other maps that are available. Unfortunately walking along such famous roads as London Road, Welford Road and Belgrave Road, for instance, is not particularly enjoyable in the first decade of the twenty-first century. Small roads that are not on direct through routes, leading to some of the remaining footpaths and pavements, are worth searching out and using. This takes time, but if you have lived in Leicester you will already be aware of some of them. Visitors will have some difficulty: even when signposts have been erected, routes should be compared with a map, and unfortunately in some areas direction signs are non-existent.

Leicester is not the easiest of areas to negotiate in a car, but happily a reasonable bus service exists. Unfortunately this city is not tourist-orientated and never has been: the City Council only pay lip service to it. The burgesses of the past and the citizens of the present have never had a real commitment to preserve the historic present in order to pass it on to the inhabitants of the future.

Many changes have taken place over the last two thousand years in this, the centre of England. The Romans made this town, named *Ratae*, part of their Empire. From the remains that have survived it must have been magnificent. To have lived in *Ratae* if you were part of the nobility would have been most civilised; not so good if you were part of the working class, a slave or a member of the Coritani, who were possibly the tribe who lived in this area when their eventual conquerers arrived. With the demise of the Roman Empire the Germanic Angles arrived, moving into central England and controlling the Romanised inhabitants; much of *Ratae* was destroyed.

The age of Arthur is steeped in mystery and legend, but how much is fact? During the period of the Knights of the Round Table who resisted the Saxons during the fifth century this area became part of the kingdom of Mercia. Eventually Leicester emerged, to be built gradually by the occupying Saxons on the site of the ruined town.

At the Jewry Wall Museum archaeologists are attempting to put together a history of this town; as the decades pass by more information is recorded. A few of the fine Roman houses have been uncovered over the last two hundred years. Without the assistance of modern techniques, a lot of important information was not recorded and is lost. Influences from the Vikings and the Danes were absorbed by a Saxon culture that gradually developed into a landscape dominated by agriculture, envied by Europe, especially by the Normans: Saxon trade was dominating parts of the continent, exporting hides, sheepskins and particularly wool. The year 1066 changed England forever: William the Conqueror invaded, his aim to control the northern European trade. He defeated Harold at the famous battle in Sussex.

The Conqueror proceeded to occupy the whole of England, dividing the areas into districts (thus creating the counties), and granting vast areas to his loyal generals. Central England became very important to national trade. Saxons did not willingly accept their occupiers' rule. Norman castles were swiftly built in all the threatened districts, in towns, villages and some hamlets. These were easily defended structures. A circular ditch was dug and the soil was stacked inside the trench, creating a mound. Inside the ditch a palisade of sharpened tree trunks was erected, producing a defensive fence. This form of circular trench defence had not changed much since the bronze-age armies defended encampments such as Borrough Hill. Did the Coritani defend any areas around Leicester before they were subjected to Roman rule?

If you visit the site of Leicester Castle, the mound that was erected still stands near the River Soar. These fortified mounds were a temporary measure, to be superseded by stone castles; few of any type have survived intact in the Midlands. Leicester Castle would have been a notable feature. Built in the year 1068 as a motte-and-bailey, a stone castle was constructed by Robert de Beaumont, first Earl of Leicester, in 1108 on an adjacent site. With the stabilisation of the countryside in the middle of the twelfth century the occupying armies of the king passed the control of vast areas of land to feudal lords. England came under the control of the Catholic Church, and of the Pope in Rome. The Augustinians commenced building Leicester Abbey in 1143, and many other places of worship were erected over the next two hundred years. Unquestionably one of the most beautiful churches was the Collegiate Church of the Annunciation of St Mary in the Newarke, which is visited by hundreds of pilgrims – today's tourists.

In 1485 Richard III, the last Plantagenet, was killed on Bosworth Field, and Henry Tudor became king. The Tudors eventually changed the course of English religion when in 1509 Henry VIII was crowned. He resented the domination of papal law and the raising of taxes for the Pope, so he created the Church of England. Henry VIII elected himself as subservient only to God, thus controlling all aspects of the country, especially as receiver of taxes. His aim was to create a vast fortune for his use as divine ruler, creating a new world empire. He needed the wealth of the church to do this, which he gained by the dissolution of the religious houses, abbeys, churches and monasteries. Britain began to achieve its position as a new empire, and this was consolidated by Henry's daughter, Elizabeth I.

Resentment against the king was stimulated in the houses of parliament, and civil war commenced in 1642 – King Charles I against the elected parliament. Leicester was the centre of this terrible war, and the town was sacked on the instructions of the king. Cromwell's commonwealth was not a successful period of English history. After the restoration of Charles II Leicester grew as a centre for trade; to gain wealth was the ambition of the burgesses of the town. The history of the ancient town was ignored, while speculative businessmen and developers looked inwards throughout the seventeenth, eighteenth and especially into the Victorian period of the nineteenth century. The Victorians have much to answer for: they destroyed so much, yet today what they created has become part of history. They also built much that has been lost in the recent modernisation of the historic town by today's civic inheritors.

Leicester was created a city in 1919 by Royal Charter, and letters patent were granted on 2 December 1926. Since that date the coat of arms was incorporated wherever possible on civic, city and legal documents, features and properties. The College of Heralds was commissioned to produce the coat of arms, the shield being surmounted by a legless wyvern.

In 1949 I enrolled in the Leicester College of Art on The Newarks – walking down Southgate Street from the bus station off Peacock Lane. This interesting Victorian street then entered The Newarks through the arches to the pavement in front of The Magazine. How can the civic engineers and planners be proud of what they have achieved in this area of their city? Modern planners often have no thought of the past. This type of abuse has been repeated throughout the city.

Let's hope the citizens who are now responsible for this fine historic city learn from the past and preserve what has survived by sound restoration, to keep interesting buildings for the future. I am an outsider looking in: for over forty years I was involved in the city and for thirty-five years I worked in and near The Newarks, admiring so much that was the best of Leicester. For two thousand years the city has suffered much, gained much, lost a lot. Let's hope that as Leicester moves through this new millennium it is governed by sound sense, and by realistic citizens.

Trevor Hickman
January 2002

1

A Market Town

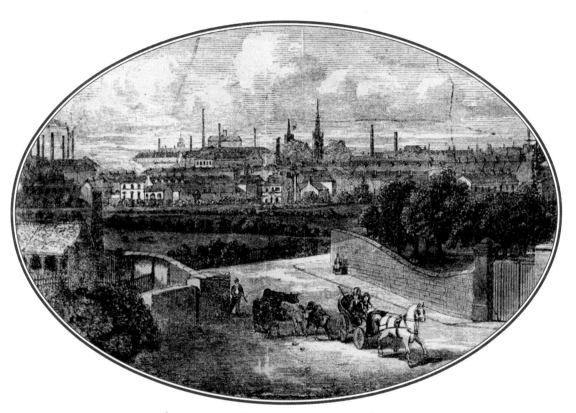

This engraving, published in 1874, illustrates the growth of a Victorian town. It is viewed from the South Fields, drawn by John Dower, printed and published by G.W. Bacon in London. In the background of the factory façade standing above the smoking town, are the spires of the churches of St Nicholas and St Martin. Markets have been held in various areas of the town for over 2,000 years. The Romans ran a market, the Danes and Saxons also sold goods in small markets, possibly commencing at the market square that is still so popular off Gallowtree Gate. When this drawing was produced the famous cattle market operated off the South Fields. I can remember visiting the weekly market especially where sheep and poultry were sold off Aylestone Road in the 1950s.

STREET MARKETS

The last Leicester Fair held in Humberstone Gate, 13 May 1904. It is interesting to note the tram lines that run along the highway. One of the main reasons why this market was closed down was the problems created by trams passing down the road.

Carriages on Humberstone Gate, 1901.

Owing to popular demand, a new fair began on the South Fields in October 1904. In this commemorative photograph, a fair, side show and the expanded market is shown, along with the sale of cattle and poultry.

CORN EXCHANGE

Leicester Corn Exchange, built in 1850 by William Flint, shown in 1903. Corn, wheat, barley and oats are being traded here. One of the leading dealers purchasing from an exchange on this site was Cooper Thornhill, Coutts & Co.'s representative. In the 1730s he became nationally famous for marketing the famous Stilton cheese. This cheese was purchased in large quantities from the cheese markets that were organised in the town. For further reading, consult my book *The History of Stilton Cheese*, Sutton Publishing 2001.

A splendid view of the Market Place, 20 May 1919. This photograph shows an open air memorial service for King Edward VII. The church choir are standing on the raised steps. What is amazing is that spectators are sitting on the roof of Simpkin and James, but above all, people are sitting on the ridge tiles above the printers, Gamble and Johnson.

THE MARKET PLACE

Leicester Market archway, designed by John Clinch and erected to the entrance on 12 March 1997.

Leicester Market, 2001. In the background stands the High Cross pillar, that was originally erected as 'The High Cross', at the entrance to the High Street.

The entrance to the Market Place with the Corn Exchange in the background, centre, *c.* 1930.

The Central building was erected in 1887 at the entrance to the Market Place. Its famous clock is surmounted with a shield and the Leicester wyvern, the town's coat of arms prior to 1919.

A bronze statue to the 5th Duke of Rutland, by sculptor Edward Davis, cast in London in 1850. Born at Belvoir Castle, the duke (1778–1857) made many generous donations to various good causes in Leicestershire. He donated 100 guineas to relieve the plight of the poor of Leicester in 1840.

A fine selection of fresh fish on display at the stall of A. & B. Peet, fish merchants.

The fish market, Leicester. A very wide variety of fresh fish is available for people living in this multi-cultural city.

Loach's stall: assorted fish and crustaceans are offered for sale.

A classic view of
Leicester market,
1905.

The Market Place, 1904, possibly
just starting to develop after the
closure of the street markets.

Leicester market, 2001. It is now considered to be the
largest covered market in Europe.

TRANSPORT

The Clock Tower, looking down Belgrave Gate in the 1930s. The features of these buildings should have been maintained. Is the Haymarket today an improvement?

The Thomas Cook building on Gallowtree Gate, built in 1894, and now occupied by B.G. Pensions Scheme. The façade features four terracotta relief panels depicting Thomas Cook's career.

A fine statue of Thomas Cook (1808–92) standing outside London Road railway station.

A relief panel recording Thomas Cook's first excursion to a temperance gathering at Loughborough, 1841.

Cook's tour to the Great Exhibition in Hyde Park, London in 1851.

Thomas Cook opened an office in Cairo in 1873 instituting steamer tours on the Nile. In 1884 he was commissioned by the British Government to provide transport down the Nile to convey troops to relieve Khartoum, which resulted in the battle of Omdurman.

In 1891 Thomas Cook celebrated its Golden Jubilee; the panel shows a train passing over the Forth Bridge.

A view of the Clock Tower just before the First World War. On the left stands Thomas Cook's office on Gallowtree Gate.

Leicester's first horse-drawn tram, standing at the Belgrave terminus in 1874. The first service ran from the Clock Tower along Belgrave Road.

The Clock Tower when the tramway was being laid in 1903. Considered by many experts to be the most complex structure in Britain, the tramway only took ten days to position on this site.

St Margarets, August 1878, with the then modern method of 'horse power'. The horse-drawn tram on the left had been running for four years.

Gallowtree Gate with the Clock Tower, leading to Belgrave Gate, 1903. Should the modern experts ever consider laying a tram system in the city sometime in the future, how long would it take?

The High Street, Leicester with a tram running to Fosse Road from the Clock Tower, c. 1930. Hoggett's the tailors can be seen on the left. Some alterations are being undertaken above the main entrance.

The opening ceremony of the newly designed 'Electric Tram Cars' that replaced the horse-drawn trams. Eleven cars are moving off to Stoneygate along the recently installed track on 18 May 1904. The mayor is in the front of tramcar no. 3. The cars were stationed on Abbey Park Road, in the corrugated structure on the right.

One of the Leicester Corporation Trams built by Dick Kerr & Co. Ltd, of London and Preston. The Brush Co. of Loughborough submitted a design that was rejected.

Tramcar no. 39 from the Belgrave Road terminal just passing the Clock Tower, 1904. There are two horse-drawn vehicles to the right and left of the car and a town employee is sweeping up some horses' deposits.

Humberstone Gate with the Bell Hotel and landlord Leonard Hunt Hargrave, *c.* 1916. On the right is car no. 40 collecting passengers from stopping points in the centre of the road.

The main tramcar depot, 1938. It had seven bays with capacity for 153 trams. This new workshop was built on Abbey Park Road. Today it is the bus depot close to the Grand Union canal.

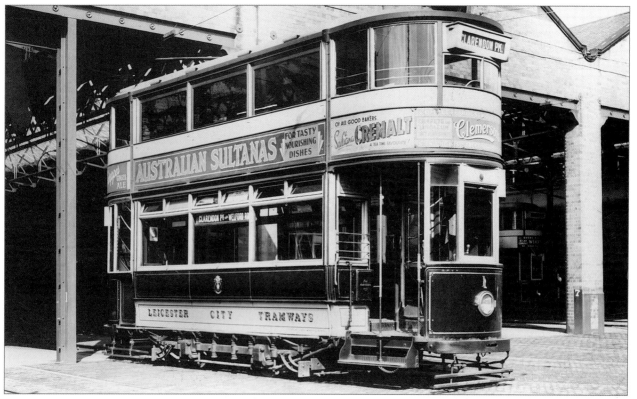

A tram built by Brush & Co., Loughborough, photographed in July 1939. A very fine example of a Leicester City tram has been restored and is exhibited at the National Tramway Museum at Crich in Derbyshire.

Humberstone Gate, 1904. On the left are three public houses: the Admiral Nelson (landlord, Reubin Staples), next to the Craven Arms (landlord, William Hill), followed by the Bell Hotel (landlord, Leonard Hunt Hargrave). Walk down the wide highway of Humberstone Gate today, and compare this photograph with the present façade. The famous market was held on this site until 13 May 1904.

Humberstone Gate, 2001, with the weighbridge on the left and what was Lewis's tower in the background. How many times has the highway been changed in the last century? It is still being ripped apart today. Perhaps they should have left some trams in the city: just imagine what a tourist attraction it would be to join a tram at the Humberstone terminal travelling through to the clock tower. After the closure of this tram route on 9 November 1949, the city planners certainly went down the wrong track. Amazingly there is now an occasional street market on this site.

Humberstone Gate, *c.* 1920. On the left is Gluckstein's and opposite is the site of Lewis's which was built between the wars and then later pulled down, leaving only the tower remaining.

Humberstone Gate, June 1938. This is a similar view to the one opposite (above). Tram nos 88, 47 and 84 can be seen. In the centre of the highway are the underground toilets.

Humberstone Gate with the Thomas Cook building on the left, 2001. The wide highway of Humberstone Gate was the site of famous street fairs. In the eighteenth century it was considered to be one of the 'Greatest Markets of England' selling corn, cattle, meat and cheese on Wednesday, Fridays and Saturdays. The speciality fairs were held on five specific dates: the eve of Palm Sunday, May Day, Midsummer Day, Michaelmas Day and 8 December.

On the left of this recent view are the weighbridge next to Humberstone House; in the background is the Lewis's tower. In the centre of the 'square blocks' is a fountain.

Above: Gallowtree Gate in the 1930s with the Lewis's tower high in the background.

Haymarket Tower, originally Lewis's Tower, today. The shopping precinct has gone but the tower has been retained.

LEICESTER STATION

Midland station, 1915. A station was opened in Leicester on 5 May 1840 followed by Campbell Street station on 1 June 1867 and London Road station on 12 June 1892.

London Road railway station in the 1930s.

London Road railway station, looking towards Granby Street, *c.* 1935.

A modern, featureless passenger train moving into the platform area, 2001. Arriving at Leicester by train is a reasonable way to start a visit to the city. Much can be seen on a one-day excursion. At certain times of the year Leicester Promotions provide a tour to discover Leicester by bus. Many of the sites mentioned in this book can be included in an itinerary. Alternatively, a full-day walk could be planned – obtain a street plan, such as an *A to Z*. To follow the route shown in this book, leave the railway station on this pre-planned circular route: London Road, Victoria Park, war memorials, Welford Road cemetery. Then walk along Filbert Street, River Soar/canal to the Bede Island development, Castle Gardens, Castle grounds, Newarke House Museum, Jain Centre, Oxford Street Antiques, Leicester Cathedral, The Guildhall, St Martin's Square, the Market Place on to Granby Street then back to London Road station. On this journey it is possible to visit some good eating houses. Some are mentioned later in the book.

The Leeds to St Pancras express, no. 5535, *Sir Herbert Wallsor KCB*, leaving Leicester, September 1938.

An LMS Johnson 3P 4–4–0, no. 721, at Leicester Sheds, January 1938.

The Sheffield to London express leaving Leicester, August 1938, being hauled by a 4–4–0 4P, compound no. 1046.

Standing in Midland station, November 1936 are 4F 0–6–0, no. 4071, and 1P 4–4–2T, no. 6660, both used extensively on the Midland line.

2

A City of Character

A statue of Simon de Montfort, standing on the Clock Tower memorial at the junction of Humberstone Gate, Gallowtree Gate, East Gate to High Street, Church Gate and Haymarket to Belgrave Gate. The Norman Simon de Montfort featured prominently in the history of Leicester. He arrived in England in 1229 and married King Henry III's sister in 1235, and he certainly did not get on with his brother-in-law. In 1239 he was invested with the Earldom of Leicester, on an inheritance from his English grandmother. A few years later he returned to his Gascon lands, now part of France.

A group of English barons were in dispute with the king over his ruling of the country, and the harsh system of taxation he had inflicted upon his subjects, As a fine soldier and statesman de Montfort had never agreed with his brother-in-law's policies, so he was chosen as the barons' leader, returning to England from Gascony in 1264, His army of barons defeated the king's army at Lewes and captured the king. Simon de Montfort was the virtual ruler of England for about twelve months. In January 1265 he formed the first English parliament with a group of barons. However, only a few months later there was a disagreement between some of the barons. Later in this year he was killed at the battle of Evesham. Simon de Montfort only lived in Leicester Castle for a few months, during the time he formed the first parliament. He made many generous grants of land to Leicester people, even though he had a very slim connection with the town and county of Leicestershire. De Montfort's name is extensively incorporated into many Leicester organisations and structures, perhaps most notably De Montfort University.

LEICESTER CASTLE

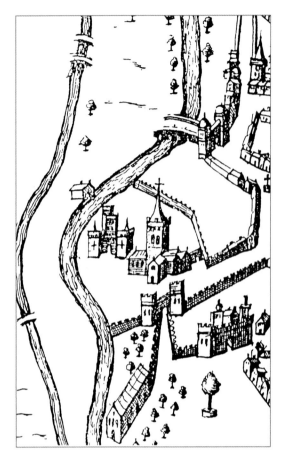

Above: An anonymous artist published this impression of the castle in the early part of the nineteenth century.

Left: A detail from John Speede's drawing of Leicester, 1610. The castle stands adjacent to the river near the water mill, with St Mary's church dominating the area below the West Gate.

The remains of the castle walls can be viewed in Castle Gardens.

An interesting drawing produced by Robert Throsby and engraved by J. Swaine in 1795. It shows the River Soar with the remains of the first castle: the 'motte and bailey' of 1068, the mound is in the centre, right. Below St Mary's church can be seen part of the remains of Leicester Castle built in 1108, incorporating the entrance to the castle cellar.

Compare this photograph published in 1904 with the engraving printed above. There are allotments, steps down to the River Soar and a bowling green in front of the motte and bailey.

The interior to the courthouse referred to as Leicester Castle in 1866, in a drawing by H. Goddard engraved by J.H. Keux.

St Mary's dominating the castle in 1905.

Left: A drawing by John Flower in 1826 of the entrance to the cellar under the castle. The site is still visible from the steps leading up the motte and bailey. The city authorities have certainly abused this excellent feature. No access to the cellar from this point is now possible, though only a few years ago it was open to the public on certain days.

Above: An early twentieth-century drawing of the steps viewed from inside the castle and leading to the entrance to the cellar.

Above: Leicester Castle yard in a drawing published in 1899.

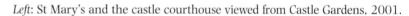

Left: St Mary's and the castle courthouse viewed from Castle Gardens, 2001.

A view of Leicester Castle yard similar to the drawing printed above, 2001.

St Mary's church with gatehouse leading to Leicester Castle yard in the 1920s.

Leaving Leicester Castle yard via Prince Rupert's gateway in the 1920s.

Richard III is associated with Leicester; indeed he is buried in the city. A monument records the fact that he was King of England from 1483 to 1485. He stayed for one night in the Old Blue Boar Inn, shown on the left in this drawing by John Flower, published in 1826. A developer demolished this famous building ten years later in 1836.

The king spent his last night in the King's Chamber in the Old Blue Boar Inn, illustrated above in a drawing by John Flower published in 1838. The next day Richard was killed at the Battle of Bosworth Field.

Above: Under the dissolution of the monasteries, Henry VIII instructed that the remains of Richard should be thrown into the River Soar. He had been buried by the Franciscan Friars in their chapel on the instructions of the victorious King Henry VII. This is reputed to be the king's coffin which stood outside the White Horse Inn on Gallowtree Gate and was used as a horse trough.

Left: King Richard III's monument now stands outside the west entrance to the castle gardens.

Leicester Castle gardens in 2001 with the recently constructed bridge leading across the river to the Bede Island development.

Left: Richard III, King of England was killed on Bosworth Field. In 1485 his body was carried back to Leicester, naked on the back of a horse for display in the Collegiate Church on the Newarke, then for burial by the Franciscan monks. This monument was erected in the Castle Gardens in 1980 by the Richard III Society. Henry VIII vandalised Richard's remains, and so have the modern Leicester populace. This monument had to be moved to a more prominent position, as his sword was repeatedly stolen.

Below: The site of Richard III's monument, 2001, with just the king's crown on the top of a post. Even after 600 years a defeated king cannot rest in peace.

RICHARD III
KING OF ENGLAND
1483 1485

Soar Point is an excellent public house and restaurant standing on the north bank of the river. On a sunny day you can sit on the raised platform outside, enjoy lunch and view the passing river traffic. It is a very busy inn during term time at De Montfort University.

Permanent residents on the river near the Leicester Castle gardens.

A canal boat moored on the quay at Leicester Castle gardens mooring site.

CARDINAL WOLSEY

The memorial to Cardinal Thomas Wolsey was erected outside the Abbey Park café in about 1979. In 1992 the memorial was vandalised and decapitated. Henry VIII failed to do this in 1530 when he had Wolsey, who was his Lord Chancellor at the time, arrested for high treason simply because the cardinal could not, or would not, sanction the divorce by the king of his first wife Catherine of Aragon.

A new head for the statue was carved by Bristol-based sculptor Mark Thompson from a block of Portland stone. Unfortunately, the head is too big for the body!

On travelling back to London from his retirement home at Cawood Thomas Wolsey (*c.* 1475–1530) stopped at Leicester Abbey, on 4 November 1530, where he died.

At last, with easy roads, he came to Leicester,
Lodg'd in the Abbey; where the reverend abbot,
With all his convent, honourably received him;
To whom he gave these words:– *O, father abbot,*
An old man, broken with the storms of state,
Is come to lay his weary bones among ye;
Give him a little earth for charity!
So went to bed: where eagerly his sickness
Pursued him still: and three nights after this,
About the hour of eight (which he himself
Foretold should be his last), full of repentance,
Continual meditations, tears, and sorrows,
He gave his honours to the world again,
His blessed part to heaven, and slept in peace.

Shakespeare, Henry VIII

LEICESTER ABBEY

The ruins of Leicester Abbey in 1826, all that remained when it was destroyed after the dissolution in 1537. The abbot, John Bourchier, surrendered all its possessions to the king. The Abbey and some of the bordering walls still survive. Above is a drawing by John Flower of all that remains of Cavendish House or Abbey Mansion; this building was subjected to considerable damage during the Civil War when Prince Rupert attacked the town in 1645. On 29 May of that year the abbey buildings were attacked by Sir Bernard Astley, his troops storming the town in the direction of St Margaret's church.

Above and right: Remains of the abbey buildings in 1900.

Cavendish House, Leicester Abbey, 1904.

Ruins in 1905.   Ruins in 2001.

ABBEY PARK

The entrance to Abbey Park from the north-west in the 1920s.

The pavilion in Abbey Park just before the beginning of the First World War in 1914.

The butterfly garden, Abbey Park, *c.* 1910.

Boating on the River Soar in Abbey Park, 1910.

The bridge across the River Soar in Abbey Park, 2001. To walk around this delightful park on a sunny day is a pleasure. I first visited this park with my parents on a memorable sunny Sunday afternoon in the summer of 1939. Much has passed under the bridge since those halcyon days.

An oil painting by George S. Ramsey of the greenhouse and gardens in Abbey Park, 1910.

Percy Geary, dairyman of 83 Noel Street, Leicester, with his horses and mobile milk steriliser. These two horse-drawn vehicles were awarded one first prize, one second prize and two third prizes at the Leicestershire Agricultural Show in 1902 and 1904 at Abbey Park.

For spectators and participants, displaying power-driven miniature ships and boats on the designated part of the pond in Abbey Park is a pleasure to all concerned, 2001.

Mute swans on Abbey Park lake, *c.* 1910.

Ninety years on, the same view of swans on the lake, possibly ancestors of the above, with the addition of Canada geese, with Simon in 2001.

The Japanese Gardens in Abbey Park before the First World War.

The Japanese Gardens in Abbey Park in the twenty-first century.

Kevin, the 7¼-inch model engine on the track in Abbey Park, a fine attraction for both young and old.

Cardinal Thomas Wolsey viewed through the gated entrance to the grounds around the café in Abbey Park. The monument was erected on this site in 1979 by Leicester City Council. The original statue was carved in 1920 for the hosiery firm, Wolsey Ltd, for its head office in King Street and it stood on the ground floor near the head of a flight of four stairs. In 1971 it was relocated to a courtyard at the Abbey Meadow premises. Eventually it was donated to Leicester City Council by Wolsey Ltd.

The children's play area in Abbey Park. There is also an interesting display of pets, birds and small animals.

Cricket being played on one of the wickets prepared in Abbey Park, for use by numerous teams.

The small children's playing area in Abbey Park.

Garden of the Muses opened by MP, and current Home Secretary, David Blunkett.

Above: Ruins erected on a small island on Abbey Park lake, *c.* 1920. This display has long since collapsed and the area is now covered with trees and bushes.

Left: 'Islands and Insulators', sculpted by Steve Geliot in painted ash on a concrete base, commissioned by Leicester City Council for Abbey Park in 1989. As it is sculpted in wood it only has a limited life expectancy. It has an archway with a sunny seascape.

A thatched bandstand, also used as a shelter for courting couples, *c.* 1920.

Two representatives of a fancy dress parade at a pageant in Abbey Park, *c.* 1920.

The Leicester/Belgrave Mela. The word mela refers to celebratory public gatherings in which travelling entertainers put on a range of attractions.

Indian folk dancers in Abbey Park, July 2001.

A group of Indian dancers with their instruments performing traditional Indian music.

The bandstand in Abbey Park with stalls displaying the richness and variety of Indian culture, July 2001.

Visitors to the Belgrave Mela sampling mouth-watering flavours from the Indian sub-continent. Many of the foods that were on offer from these stalls can be purchased along 'The Golden Mile' seven days a week.

The fair in Abbey Park, 2001.

Billy Bates's Fun Fair at Abbey Park, July 2001.

Visitors to the Mela enjoying the fun fair with a very wide variety of attractions, July 2001.

LEICESTER CATHEDRAL

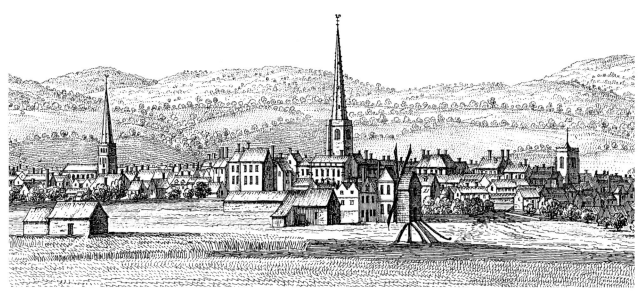

St Martin's church, 1743. To the right stands All Saints' church and to the left St Nicholas's church, from an engraving by Samuel and Nathaniel Buck. St Martin's was created a cathedral in 1926.

Above: One of the windows in Leicester Cathedral, *c.* 1930.

Right: The noble tower and spire. Compare this with the spire featured in the centre of the engraving at the top of the page. The tower and spire deteriorated and between 1862 and 1867 it was rebuilt by Brandon, the Victorian architect.

An interesting view of the medieval cathedral, *c.* 1920. Spend some time walking around this fine old building; perhaps search out its history. The tower has a ring of bells rung to celebrate many historic occasions, such as coronations and victories in the past. On record are three interesting dates: 3 June 1814 – Peace with France! 22 September – Victory over the Americans and the destruction of Washington! and 8 July 1815 – Lord Wellington parades through Paris!

The chapel of the Leicestershire regiments. A memorial is on view – a magnificent bound record of all those people from Leicestershire who were killed or died for the country.

The Vaughan Porch, the entrance to the Cathedral Church of St Martin. The porch is named in memory of the Vaughans who served the church successively as vicars throughout most of the nineteenth century.

Above the south entrance are nine statues. They are (left to right): **St George** in the niche on the far left. **Guthlac** (d. 716), a Saxon, leaving Leicester to give up his life of violence to become a hermit in the fens at Crowland. Having taken holy orders he gave his life to God. Leicester was first made a diocese with Guthlac as the first bishop in 680. **Hugh of Lincoln**, Bishop of Lincoln in the early years of the Norman conquest, when Leicester was then part of the diocese of Lincoln. Hugh founded a Carthusian monastery. Later as bishop he began the building of Lincoln Cathedral. **Robert Grosseteste**, a great scholar, was appointed Archdeacon of Leicester. He was a popular nationalist who supported the king against the financial demands of the pope. **John Wycliffe** was a famous Oxford scholar who encouraged the first translation of the Bible from Latin into English. His followers were known as Lollards. He was exiled to Lutterworth church where he died in 1384. Later his bones were dug up, burnt and thrown into the River Swift. He preached in St Martin's. He was known as the 'Morning Star of the Reformation' before the break from Rome. **Henry Hastings**, was the 3rd Earl of Huntingdon and a leading Puritan, He had a Leicester home in Lords Place in the High Street which is now the site of the Shires shopping centre. **William Chillingworth** (b. 1602) was an Oxford theologian and nephew of Archbishop Laud. Appointed Master of Wyggeston Hospital he lectured at St Martin's. He became chaplain to the Royalist Army in the Civil War in 1644 and later died as prisoner of the Roundheads. **William Conner Magee**, Bishop of Peterborough in the nineteenth century. He was appointed the first suffragan bishop of Leicester, which was then in the Peterborough diocese. He encouraged the building of many of Leicester's Victorian churches and church schools. In 1888 Magee became Archbishop of York. **St Martin** is in the niche on the right.

THE GUILDHALL

The Guildhall, The Old Town Hall, *c.* 1900, standing on St Martin's West, with plastered exterior walls. The whole building was subject to a major restoration when the exterior plaster was removed between 1922 and 1926. This building had remained empty since the opening of the new Town Hall in 1876.

The Guildhall at the time of the 1920s restoration. Originally built for the Corpus Christi Guild, founded in 1343, this structure is on a courtyard plan. It is timber-framed on a stone base. The great hall may have been built in 1344.

A splendid view of the Guildhall and the spire and tower of St Martin's from Guildhall Lane.

From the courtyard of the Guildhall before restoration in the 1920s.

The courtyard in the 1920s.

Left: A gibbet that hangs in one of the cells that were laid out in 1840 when the police station was established in the Town Hall. James Cook, a bookbinder, murdered one of his customers and was hanged for his trouble, suspended from this gibbet off the South Fields in August 1832. Possibly he bound or restored some of the books that are stored in the library (above) that were transferred from St Martin's belfry in 1632. This photograph of the Town Library was taken in about 1900.

Right: A splendid fireplace in the Guildhall, *c.* 1900, with a ducking stool and King Charles I's chair.

The fireplace in the library, *c.* 1905. The Town Library was first mentioned in 1587 and is one of the oldest in the country. Only Bristol and Norwich have older town libraries.

THE NEWARKE

Gateway to The Newarke, by John Flower, 1826. To the right of this building was the Magazine which was destroyed in the 1960s, as it was no longer used for military purposes. Part of the area became the Southgate Street–Oxford Street underpass.

An interesting view of the turret gateway by John Flower, 1826. Used as a private house, with considerable character, today it is maintained in isolation at a road junction.

Prince Rupert's gateway from The Newarke leading into Leicester Castle Yard with the spire of St Mary's in the background, c. 1920.

The Gateway and the Magazine on The Newarkes, 1916. In the background stands the Princess Charlotte public house, 8 Oxford Street; Mrs Elizabeth Berry was the landlady at this time.

This late 1920s photograph was taken at an unusual angle; it shows the edge of the Magazine looking towards the entrance of the Gateway.

A 1914 view of Prince Rupert's gateway, St Mary's church and the Chantry House, built in 1511 for William Wygston and used by priests from the Collegiate church, stands opposite.

The spire of St Mary's, the Magazine gateway and the underpass. Compare this modern view with the one at the top of page 68.

A museum display in the Newarke House Museum of a framework knitter, 1980.

The Newarke, 2001. On the right is the Newarke House Museum, originally two buildings built in the sixteenth and seventeenth centuries but later brought together as one to form the museum. In the centre background is the historic Magazine, across the underpass. Planners elected by the city councillors in the 1960s have a lot to answer for – particularly the destruction of this historic site in the name of progress.

Newarke House Museum is well worth a visit, and contains a fine record of the city. The house was built in part for the Skeffington family in 1600.

An engraving published in the eighteenth century of the Collegiate Church of the Annunciation of St Mary that stood opposite Chantry House. This magnificent church was built in 1345, but it was demolished in 1548 during the ongoing scheme instigated in the reign of King Henry VIII for the dissolution of religious houses.

Below: 'The Thorn taken from the Crown of Jesus' displayed in the Collegiate church. Thousands of pilgrims visited the church to pay homage to this religious artefact.

Below, right: The remains of the Collegiate church, restored and preserved in the basement of De Montfort University's Hawthorne building.

Technical and Art School on The Newarke, 1904; it is now the Hawthorne building. This indicates the completion of the second phase together with the Gateway school, on the left. The art school was completed in various stages as money became available. I enrolled into the art school in 1948, spending many happy and interesting hours in the bookbinding department: the two large ground-floor windows indicate the classrooms, far left.

The Magazine gateway on The Newarke leading to Southgate Street from Oxford Street, *c*. 1916. On the right stands the public house Duke of York, whose landlord was Alfred Budett. I have fond memories of walking down Southgate Street from the bus station to the College of Art just after the Second World War; at that time little or no change had been made. My old friend Don Humberston has fond memories of visiting the café 'Greasy Joe's' on the left of the photograph for an egg on toast when he was an apprentice, as did many students visiting the colleges close by. It is virtually impossible to compare this view today with what planners have left us.

The Newarke again, *c*. 1916. The Magazine gateway in the background with soldiers of the Leicestershire regiment leaving for Flanders, passing E. Garner & Co., printers, bookbinders and machine rulers at 9 Newarke Street.

ST MARGARET'S

Above: A tram approaching St Margaret's church, 1904. The church has what is considered to be one of the finest perpendicular towers in Leicestershire. Saxon remains have been uncovered in this area; some are on display in the church. One of the arcades in the earliest part of the church was built in about 1200 and the tower is thought to have been constructed in about 1440. Through many centuries changes and alterations have been made. *Right*: The magnificent tower of St Margaret's.

Left: St Margaret's church stands on St Margaret's Way.

Right: Some excellent carvings, along with a fine descriptive memorial are featured on the magnificent tomb of Lord Rollo who died in Leicester in 1765. As Brigadier-General in 1761 he led his troops in various actions on islands in the Caribbean.

St Margaret's bus station on Burley's Way. For a tourist visiting Leicester this is an ideal point at which to start a tour by bus – obtain an up-to-date timetable and select an itinerary. Alternatively, much of the city can be viewed on foot, commencing at this bus station. Walk along St Margaret's Way past the church, take the footpath into Abbey Park near the sports ground that also leads to the towpath on the Grand Union Canal. From here very interesting walks can be chosen: along the canal to Belgrave Hall Museum, returning via the River Soar, through Abbey Park, and past Abbey pumping station and the National Space Centre. All are within easy walking distance on a whole day itinerary.

The City Council welcomes you to the city at St Margaret's bus station.

Double-decker buses lined up in the bus station, 2001.

3
Historic Highways

The Memorial Clock Tower on the Haymarket in 1903 prior to the electrification of the tramway system. Thomas Cook's head offices are on the left on Gallowtree Gate. The horse-drawn tram on the right is moving towards a group of trams and horses that are standing on East Gate, which leads to Cheapside and High Street.

The foundation stone to the tower was laid on 16 March 1868, by John Burton, on the site of Coal Hill clearly indicated on the plan printed on page 73. In October 1867 a petition was submitted to the corporation to build an island to regulate traffic at the Coal Hill site. The Council agreed to pay all costs in December of that year. A competition was organised, 'The Haymarket Memorial Structure' was awarded to John Burton & Son. It was decided that four notable historic Leicester people should be displayed; the sculptor appointed was Samuel Barfield. By December 1868 the whole tower was completed. Dismay was expressed by many as soon as the selected statues were erected. Many people thought that Lady Jane Gray should have been included instead of one of the lesser-known individuals. The selected four are: Simon de Montfort (*c.* 1208–65), hardly a Leicestershire person; William Wigston (1467–1536), a native of Leicester and was mayor in 1499 and 1510, and a very generous person who donated considerable amounts of money to charitable causes in Leicester; Sir Thomas White (1492–1567), a native of Reading who had no personal connection with Leicester, though through a specific trust that he founded local trustees receive money for the poor; finally Gabriel Newton (1683–1762), a publican who owned the Horse and Trumpet near the High Cross. On his death he left the not inconsiderable sum of £3,250 for the use of schooling and education for boys living in Leicester.

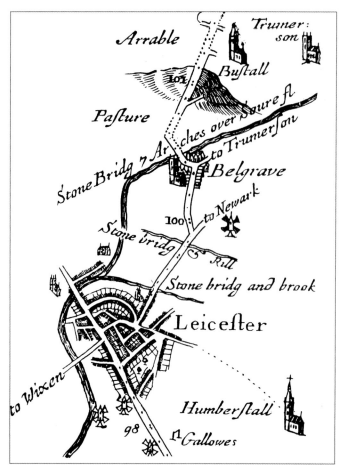

A detail from John Ogilby's strip map of 1675 showing the London Road, which was 98 miles from London. These strip maps were considered to be fairly accurate, principally designed for military use by officers on horseback leading troops around the country. All high points that could be sighted from a person on the back of a horse riding on the highway, such as windmills, gallows, churches, especially those with high towers and steeples, are marked. Bridges were also included. It is interesting to note that considerable open countryside existed between Leicester and Belgrave, with the particular reference to the stone bridge with seven arches across the River Soar (see page 105).

An early nineteenth-century view of the county gaol on Welford Road, drawn and engraved from a view beyond Bede House Meadows. The River Soar would appear to be in flood in front of St Mary's church.

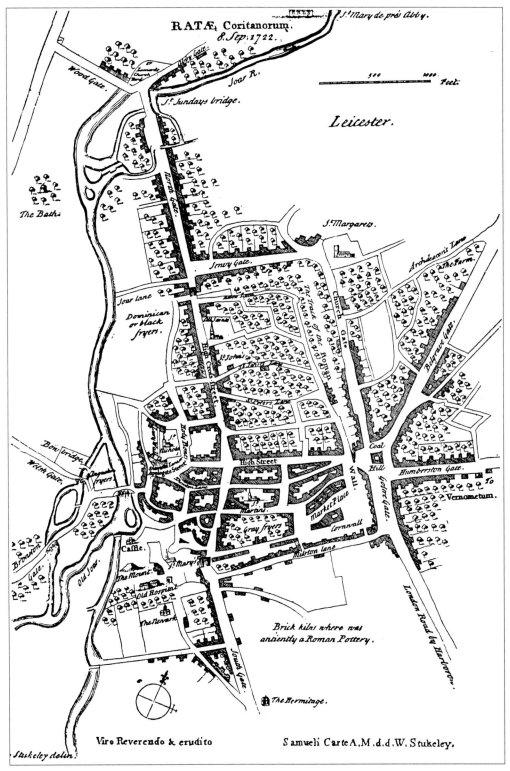

A plan of Leicester drawn in 1722 by Samuel Carte and engraved by W. Stukeley. It is a strange map, influenced by the past and including the prominent features in the eighteenth century. According to this map the castle and the collegiate church still stand. Coal Hill is clearly evident. This was the site where coal was delivered to be stacked and sold, well into the nineteenth century, on the site of what is now the Clock Tower.

THOMAS COOK

Thomas Cook (1808–92) standing outside Leicester railway station on the corner with Station Street and London Road. He was born at Melbourne in Derbyshire and was apprenticed to a wood turner. He moved to Loughborough then lived in Rutland and became deeply involved in the Temperance Association. He commissioned a special train, the first publicly advertised train in England, to take 570 people from Leicester to Loughborough with a return fare of 1s per person. With this success he decided to turn his efforts into a full-time business. Moving to Leicester, he entered into a partnership with the Midland Railway Company. With his son, who became a partner in 1864, they moved their head office to London, and became pioneers in the world of travel and tourism.

This bronze statue, designed by James Butler, was unveiled by Thomas Cook, the founder's great-great grandson, on Friday 14 January 1994.

LONDON ROAD

The Midland Railway station on London Road, 1904. Two trams are delivering passengers to the station precinct. The first platform for passengers was opened on this site on 12 June 1892.

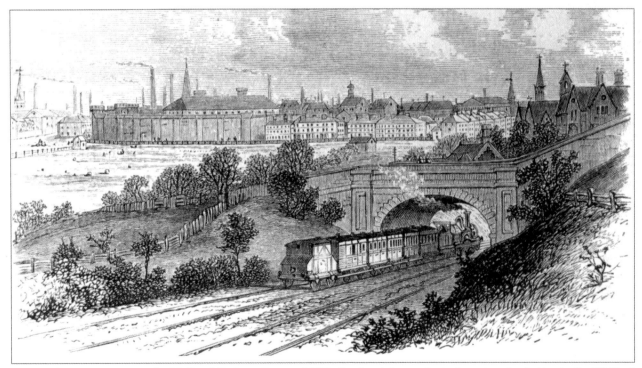

Approaching Leicester on the Midland Railway line, *c.* 1870. On the right as the train enters the bridge is the Welford Road cemetery. The formidable County Gaol stands in the background off Freemans Common, leading to London Road, the Campbell Street station.

A classic view of Edwardian Leicester on London Road, 1904. Two splendid trams are in line with a chauffeur-driven horse-drawn vehicle on the right. The leading tram carries an advertisment for Tylers boots, at 48–50 Market Place, Leicester.

Compare this view taken in 2001 of the Midland Railway station with the one at the top of page 75.

A city dominated by cars. Previous pages have featured the trams conveying passengers around the city. Over the decades the elected politicians and appointed officers have lacked vision. They should have improved the tramway system, not destroyed it. I can just remember the experience of making a short journey on a tram. In the background stand the offices of the *Leicester Mercury*, with the banner 'Regional Newspaper of the Year': a newspaper with vision, though it has often been ignored by local politicians.

Tram no. 61 on the way to Stoneygate up London Road, *c.* 1920.

'TANKY' SMITH

Top Hat Terrace, 113–19 London Road, built by James Francis Smith in honour of his famous father, Francis 'Tanky' Smith, who was one of the first detectives to be elected on the formation of the newly created Leicester Police Force in 1836. On retirement he set himself up as a private detective. Almost immediately he was commissioned to find the High Sheriff of Leicestershire, James Beaumont Winstanley, who had gone missing on a tour of Europe. He found his corpse floating in the River Moselle. Smith was noted for his disguises. His nickname 'Tanky' was given for his habit of tapping disorderly people on their head with his stick – 'tanking'. The sixteen heads carved in stone displayed on the front of this building represent some of the very many disguises he adopted in his brilliant career and time in the police force.

City of Leicester

Top Hat Terrace
built by

FRANCIS "TANKY" SMITH
d. 1888

Leicester's first private detective

Each of the sixteen carved heads on the building represent Tanky Smith in one of his many disguises

A blue plaque on the wall of Top Hat Terrace commemorates the life and work of 'Tanky' Smith. It should say built in honour of Francis 'Tanky' Smith.

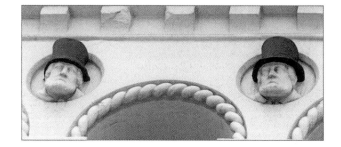 

Fourteen of the sixteen carved heads representing some of 'Tanky' Smith's many disguises.

THE MARQUIS OF WELLINGTON

An exceptionally fine public house, the Marquis of Wellington, standing at 139 London Road and now part of Everards Brewery estates, opened as a hostelry in 1893. The landlord in 1899 was T. Brandeth. The major restoration was completed in 1907. It is well worth a visit to enjoy some fine ale and admire the photographs and illustrations that are on display.

Arthur Wellesley (1769–1852), 1st Duke of Wellington. In 1796 at the rank of colonel he was posted to India to learn his craft of soldiering. In 1805 he was awarded a knighthood and elected as an MP, and later, in 1808, he was given command of the British Expeditionary Force sent to fight Bonaparte's armies in Portugal. He developed his famous military tactic known as 'scorched earth' policy. His most famous defeat of Napoleon was at the Battle of Waterloo in 1815; the year before he had been created the 1st Duke of Wellington.

The bars in the Marquis of Wellington. Clearly visible are some of the historic photographs of Leicester.

The courtyard in 2001, a pleasant location to enjoy a light midday meal.

Right: Don enjoying a 'light lunch' in the bar of this excellent public house, 2001.

SILVER STREET

The Globe Public House on Silver Street was opened in about 1720. Everards Brewery purchased it in 1887.

Maynard and Bradley, a second-hand bookshop on Silver Street, is well worth a visit for anyone interested in books on local history.

GRANBY STREET

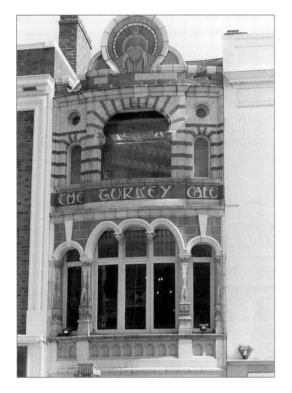

Above: An engraving from the letter heading used at the Grand Hotel, a limited company in 1904. *Left*: The Turkey Café on Granby Street was built on the instructions of the architect Arthur Wakerley (1862–1931) who was elected mayor at the age of thirty-five.

Granby Street with tram lines running along the cobbled street, 1905. The Grand Hotel is on the left.

Granby Street, *c.* 1930.

Granby Street in the twenty-first century.

GALLOWTREE GATE

Gallowtree Gate: the junction of Horsefair Street to Halford Street, *c.* 1910. F.W. Woolworth is on the right with an open-top tram moving towards the Clock Tower.

W.H. Smith on Gallowtree Gate on the right. There is an entrance to this shop from the Market Place.

Tramcar no. 102 travelling down Gallowtree Gate from the Clock Tower in about 1920. The tram was built by the Electric Car Company in 1913.

A similar view to the one above, *c*. 1910, looking into the top of the open-top tramcar travelling down Gallowtree Gate via the Clock Tower, Belgrave Gate and Belgrave Road going on to Melton Road.

Gallowtree Gate with the Thomas Cook building on the left, 1960s.

Humberstone Gate leading to the Clock Tower with the Thomas Cook building and Gallowtree Gate on the left.

APPLEGATE

Wygston's House on Applegate, Leicester. It was built in the sixteenth century by the family of Roger Wigston (or Wygston) who died in 1507; he had been elected Lord Mayor on three occasions. This photograph features a display of glass, originally painted-glass windows, part of a gallery of twenty-nine panels. They were removed in 1824 by the then owner, Richard Stevens. Thomas North purchased those that had survived from the estate of the owner for £17, and donated them to the Leicester Museum in 1917. Featured in this are the borough arms and crest, with a four-legged wyvern (see page 113). Now the building is the Learning Exchange, NCBI, WEA.

Carey's Cottage was named after William Carey, a minister at Harvey Lane chapel and scholar of oriental studies, who became a missionary in India in the 1790s. The cottage was demolished by the city council as a result of the 1960s highway development. Carey's Close is off Applegate.

On the demolition of Carey's Cottage these two carved stones were erected on the inside wall of the garden at Wygston's House.

HIGH STREET

Many changes have taken place on the High Street. 'The Shires', a modern development, is a credit to the city planners. A well-designed tower leads to a fine shopping complex, and retains some of the character of the Huntingdon Tower on the High Street that was demolished very early in the twentieth century.

The Imperial Playhouse, *c.* 1916. The manager was Leslie Stanford. The building stood on this site until well after the Second World War when it was known as the Cameo Cinema.

Huntingdon Tower, May 1902 – just before it was demolished. This carved stone plaque is displayed near part of the Shires on the High Street, known as the 'Tower House', 'Lord's Place', 'Reynolds Place' and 'Huntingdon Tower'. The original Huntingdon Tower was built in about 1500 and in 1505 it was owned by Richard Reynold. The original structure had two towers to the grand main entrance. Later it was owned by Henry, 3rd Earl of Huntingdon (1536–95). His statue is the fourth from the left in the group of seven figures standing above the main entrance to the cathedral. Mary Queen of Scots was imprisoned here en route to Coventry, and in the sixteenth century Kings James I, Charles I, Charles II and Prince Rupert stayed in the house. The Shires centre stands well – if only the Huntingdon Tower had been maintained and restored!

The High Street, 2001. The Huntingdon Tower plaque is just visible, centre right. The Shires shopping centre has been open since 1991. Open seven days a week, it offers extensive car parking, free after 6 p.m. National retailers are housed in the complex, such as Next, Virgin, Debenhams, Burtons and Waterstones, to name but a few.

Children's entertainment.

The entrance to the Shires from Church Gate.

WELFORD ROAD

The junction of Welford Road and Aylestone Road looking south, 1904. Over the centuries Welford Road was a route north for kings to the town. King Charles I travelled this way. To the south lies the Civil War battlefield of Naseby near the village of Welford. This battle eventually changed the course of English history.

On Welford Road stands the imposing county gaol, *c.* 1905. It was built by the county surveyor, W. Parsons, between 1825 and 1828.

A marvellous view of Welford Road, 1904. Tramcar no. 48 is moving up the road from Welford Place; and an early motorcar, a horse-drawn carriage and numerous bicycles are on the highway. On the right is the Bricklayers Arms, with James Walter Sweet the publican, retailing beers made at the Beeston Brewery Co. Ltd. Next door at no. 80 is the branch post office of Walter Warwick Waddington who was also a stationer, newsagent and tobacconist.

A similar view to the photograph published above with tramcar no. 27 on its way to Aylestone.

AYLESTONE ROAD

Tramcar no. 23 travelling down Aylestone Road, 1904. The Aylestone service began on 5 September 1904. First on the left is Napier Terrace. No. 23 was owned by William Cornelius Herbert and contained lock-up shops and an off-licence. Next door is the Bedford Hotel; the licensee was Edwin Wortley. At no. 19 stands the Freemans Hotel, so named after Freemans Common, off Aylestone Road. The licensee of the hotel was Edward Clayton.

Compare this view taken in 2001 with the one above. The three main buildings still stand, and are part of the Victorian and Edwardian history of Leicester. The Victory public house was originally Napier Terrace.

WEST BRIDGE

Buildings on and at the West Bridge, *c.* 1820, drawn by John Flower (1793–1861), a very fine artist and local historian. The picture shows the entrance to the town from the west. The River Soar was divided, forming a large island to the west of the town. The West Bridge was linked via the highway to the famous Bow Bridge. Richard III made two journeys across this bridge in 1485 on his way to the Battle of Bosworth – he was eventually killed on Redmore Plain. He returned across this bridge, naked across the back of a horse, eventually to be interred in Grey Friars Abbey.

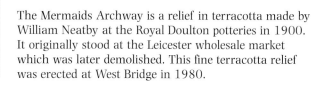

The Mermaids Archway is a relief in terracotta made by William Neatby at the Royal Doulton potteries in 1900. It originally stood at the Leicester wholesale market which was later demolished. This fine terracotta relief was erected at West Bridge in 1980.

John Flower published two fine drawings of West Bridge; this view details one of the houses actually erected on the bridge. Unbelievably this magnificent historic bridge was demolished in 1841.

The West Bridge area was changed completely when the Great Central Railway was built through the west of the town in the late nineteenth century. The first railway line to pass through West Bridge was the Leicester to Swannington line opened on 17 July 1832. This wood engraving was published at the opening. It features the passengers' station on the banks of the navigation, a barge on the canal and a steam engine on the track.

West Bridge, a Victorian construction opened in 1891 by the Mayor, William Kempson, Aldermen Henry Chambers and John Underwood and the Town Clerk E.G. Mabey. There are some fine carvings on the decorative battlements of the four octagonal piers representing medieval characters.

Two octagonal piers on West Bridge before the First World War. Excavations and alterations are taking place on the site of Leicester Castle between the bridge and St Mary de Castro church.

New Walk

Take a stroll down New Walk from University Road to Welford Place. This walkway through the centre of the city it is unique. It was laid out as a promenade called the Queens Walk by the corporation in 1785. Most of its length was then outside the old town. Houses along the route were built and some, mainly nineteenth-century, were demolished to make way for twentieth-century offices such as these. Planners seemed to consider them worth building!

The Museum on New Walk, opened by the corporation in 1848.

New Walk and West Walk, *c.* 1905. Considerable alterations have taken place off New Walk, yet it still retains much of its eighteenth-century character. At the end of New Walk is Welford Place, the main offices of Leicester City Council. For information relevant to much of the contents of this book contact the Living History Unit, Arts & Leisure Department, Leicester City Council, New Walk Centre, Welford Place, Leicester, LE1 6ZG.

Edwardian ladies strolling down New Walk, *c.* 1905.

A splendid view of the cast-iron columns in New Walk, *c.* 1910.

An interesting view of a church parade in New Walk, *c.* 1905.

Compare this modern view with the ones opposite.

A pair of cannon from the Crimean War on display in front of the entrance to the museum, 2001.

THE GOLDEN MILE

The Palace Theatre of Varieties at 24–6 Belgrave Gate, 1925. The manager was Trueman Towers at that time. At the side of this building stands the Floral Hall Picture Theatre, the manager of which was W.P. Carter. I have memories of walking down the strange corridor to this cinema with friends to sit in 'The Flea Pit' in the 1950s. In the centre background stands the spire to the Victorian church of St Mark's on Belgrave Road.

Belgrave Gate, *c.* 1930. It now leads to 'The Golden Mile' that stretches from Belgrave Gate down Belgrave Road to Melton Road and Loughborough Road. It is known as 'The Golden Mile' because the Indian wares on sale in its shops sparkle in the Sunday sun.

Compare this view taken in 2001 with the two opposite.

The taxi rank outside the Haymarket centre and theatre on Belgrave Gate with the splendid Victorian church of St Mark's standing in the background on Belgrave Road. This church contains some fine paintings by the Scottish artist James Eadie-Reid that show the Leicester class struggle in the 1920s. The church was built between 1870 and 1872; considerable extensions were added in 1904.

Belgrave Road, 18 May 1904, showing the new tramway with a horse-drawn cart.

The roundabout leading from the junction with Belgrave Gate, Langton Street, Belgrave Road, Bedford Street South and Charles Street, 2001.

The Tollgate on Loughborough Road in Belgrave was abolished on 1 November 1878. This site became the terminus of tramcars travelling along this route. The first horse-drawn tramcar left this site for the Clock Tower on 24 December 1874, four years before the tollgate was abolished.

Rope makers and tent suppliers, Belgrave Gate, 1901.

The bridge across the River Soar in Belgrave, *c.* 1905. On visiting Belgrave Hall it is worth walking around Belgrave Gardens to examine part of the remains of this ancient bridge, which still stands near the modern bridge that carries the Thurcaston Road across the navigation.

The Belgrave Road on leaving the northbound Belgrave Flyover, 2001.

Commercial properties on the Belgrave Road, 2001.

Indian products on sale in 'The Golden Mile', Belgrave Road, 2001.

The Belgrave Road in the twenty-first century. Visitors interested in fine clothing, jewellery and food influenced by Indian culture should spend some time in this area of the city.

Two tramcars at the junction of Loughborough Road, Melton Road and Belgrave Road, *c.* 1930.

Compare this view, taken in 2001, with the view printed above. Amazingly, a number of properties have not been extensively altered.

This building at 98–100 Melton Road was known as the Coliseum Picture Theatre when this façade was built in the 1930s. It joined many fine cinema palaces, with Art Deco features. This is one of the very few that remains in Leicestershire. It was converted for use as a bingo hall, but now it is once again a fine cinema and a centre for Bollywood films.

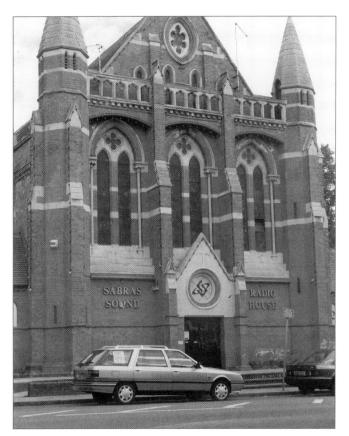

Sabras Sound Radio House in Belgrave is a centre for Indian culture. It was originally the church of St Michael and All Angels.

An historic view of Belgrave Road in 1904. St Mark's stands high in the background as tramcar no. 73 passes three horse-drawn vehicles. The tram carries an advertisements for E.F. Carr, tailor, who was at 70 Belgrave Road, on the right. Perhaps this was a posed photograph.

4

Civic Duty

A view of the Town Hall on the municipal square in the 1930s. There have been conflicting thoughts on the development of the city of Leicester since it was formed in 1919. Many people, including myself, consider that more of the history of this fine old Midlands town should have been preserved with thought for the future. From the medieval period onward the town was mainly concerned with finance through industry. History for education and tourism play a very small part in the town's progress, and unfortunately the elected councillors and officers still adopt a monetary gain policy. It could be considered unfair to view this city with others in the Midlands as it does maintain a position in commerce. It is always easy to be critical when you do not sit in the 'hot seat'.

Overleaf: A fine plan of Leicester drawn in 1828 by A. Cockshow.

1919

Horsefair Street, showing the municipal buildings before Leicester was created a city in 1919.

SEMPER   EADEM.

The coat of arms prior to this date was a shield emblazoned with the arms of Robert Fitz Parnel, Earl of Leicester, who accompanied Richard I on his crusade to the Holy Land. When adopted by the burgesses of Leicester, a wyvern was added. The earliest record of it is on a deed dated 1343. Panels were painted on the city trams after the coat of arms was granted letters patent on 2 December 1926. This drawing was produced in 1927 by students. There is a shield decorated with a flower, possibly a pimpernel, containing ermine (stoat) tails – on the breasts of the two coroneted backward-looking lions there are similar flowers. The shield supports a knight's helmet surrounded by a wreath, surmounted by a legless wyvern. The wyvern of the Tudor kings had two legs. The Leicester wyvern is a slippery customer: a dragon-like lizard with a pointed tail. The College of Heralds artist had a very jaundiced view of the town of Leicester. The town witnessed the killing of two kings: the last Plantaganet and a Stuart. Simon de Montfort attacked his king and Henry VIII destroyed many of the fine religious buildings in the town. The burgers supported Parliament in the Civil War. History is recorded in part; frankly it should have displayed two rampant lions or tigers and a wyvern with legs. Simon de Montfort set up the first parliament and was put to death. Whatever the views of the townspeople may have been they certainly were not cowardly. They chose the motto: *Semper Eadem* – always the same, used by Queen Elizabeth I. From the 1930s until well into the 1960s academics in the College of Art continued to comment disapprovingly about the way the city coat of arms was presented by the College of Heralds.

A Tudor wyvern (right) and a Leicester wyvern (far right), legless!

Town Hall and square, 2001. The fountain was designed by Francis J. Hames and unveiled by Sir Israel Hart on 24 September 1879.

A postcard franked on 8 April 1906, depicting the town arms. The town arms should have been ignored in 1919. Two wyverns with two legs and a shield containing three lions passant (walking on four legs) were on the seal of Henry, Earl of Lancaster, who died in 1361. The cinqfoils were on the seal of the Borough of Leicester in 1334. From this town arms the city coat of arms were produced. They were criticised when submitted to the councillors by various artists and designers and individuals working in education in the city. The record of past borough coats of arms was excluded, especially the Wigston windows.

Many inhabitants of the recently formed city consider that tigers should have been chosen by the heraldic artist when drawing the coat of arms for the city in the early 1920s. This regiment served the city and county well from when it was formed in the seventeenth century, as the seventeenth of foot, and was awarded the tiger on its badge in 1825 by King George IV.

WAR MEMORIALS

The South African war memorial was erected in 1909 to commemorate over 300 soldiers from Leicestershire who gave their lives in the Boer War (1899-1902). This memorial was designed by John Breedon Everard; the sculptor was Joseph Corsland McClure. The three bronzes on the pedestals on the monument are Grief, Peace and War. Field Marshal Lord Grenfell is saluting the dead after he had unveiled the monument on Thursday 1 July 1909 in the municipal square.

McClure's bronze, 'Peace'. This splendid monument stands on the corner of Horsefair Street and Every Street.

The temporary war memorial for the First World War was erected in Town Hall Square, and unveiled by the 8th Duke of Rutland on Thursday 28 June 1917. They weren't to know that the war still had over a year to run before the Armistice. Extra space on the memorial was needed; the lettering was executed by students from Leicester College of Arts and sculptor Joseph Herbert Morcam. It was suggested that a permanent memorial should be erected in place of the fountain, but this was overruled. After the Lutyens memorial had been erected in Victoria Park in 1925 this was demolished during the winter of 1926/7.

MUNICIPAL BUILDING

A summer scene in Town Hall Square, *c.* 1905. Hames's fountain is seen here with its four Assyrian winged lions supporting the main structure.

A winter scene in Town Hall Square, *c.* 1905, from the junction of Bishop Street and Every Street.

WELFORD ROAD CEMETERY

An advertisement published in 1900 offered a vast selection of monuments that could be erected in the Welford Road cemetery. A walk through this graveyard is extremely interesting for local people who are researching their family history, as it is the last resting place for many of the citizens of Leicester.

Tombs, monuments, crosses and gravestones are laid out in the cemetery, which was opened in 1850.

A splendid tomb standing in Welford Road cemetery, 2001.

The war memorial erected in the Welford Road cemetery behind the graves of those soldiers who died in England serving their country and were associated with Leicestershire. The inscriptions on the monument indicate all those soldiers who were interred in front of the memorial, some in mass graves. Each person is indicated with a number on his plot. Left to right: Dennis Humberston, Andrew Humberston, Robert Humberston, Wendy Humberston, August 1997. Robert indicates his grandad's name, interred in plot number two. Samuel Andrew Humberston died on 15 November 1918, having joined up in the Leicestershire Regiment.

BELGRAVE HALL

Belgrave Hall was built between 1713 and 1715 by Edmund Cradock. It is a square-built construction, with a chequered pattern façade of red and blue bricks. It is three storeys high with a very plain parapet obscuring the triple-pitched roof.

The main entrance to Belgrave Hall on the junction of Thurcaston Road and Church Road in Belgrave. It is reputed to house the ghost of Belgrave.

John Flower produced this drawing of the Old Hall, Belgrave, which was published in the 1820s. During the seventeenth century it was owned by the Earls of Huntingdon. It was destroyed in about 1848 when a new road was laid through Belgrave to Red Hill.

The kitchen in Belgrave Hall, *c.* 1920. The best way to view the hall is with an organised tour. Contact the curator, through the Living History Unit, Arts and Leisure Department, Leicester City Council.

JEWRY WALL

St Nicholas's church at the Jewry
Wall off Holy Bones, *c*. 1910.

Jewry Wall at the site of the Roman Public
Baths, 2001. Excavated in the 1930s, the
baths date from about AD 130.

Holy Bones, *c*. 1890. Visit the Guru Nanak Sikh
Museum at 9 Holy Bones, Leicester.

A very fine drawing by John Flowers of the Jewry Wall facing St Nicholas's church in the 1820s. The front wall of the Roman basilica is shown, again dating from the second century AD.

This view from June 1927 looking towards St Nicholas Street is similar to the drawing above. Samuel Key's grocery shop, no. 56, is clearly visible.

Roman arches on Jewry Wall in 1908, photographed from the south side of St Nicholas's church.

Jewry Wall with St Nicholas's church shown shortly after the extensive excavation in the 1930s now the archaeological site viewed from the impressive Jewry Wall Museum. The museum was built on the instructions of Trevor Dannatt between 1960 and 1962 and holds a very fine collection of archaeological specimens and displays. *Above, right*: This display in the museum exhibits the remains of a young Saxon lady dating from about AD 500. Her grave was discovered at Glen Parva in 1866 and contained a large selection of ornaments and possessions.

Two photographs of a Roman pavement originally discovered when a house was being built on Jewry Wall Street in 1832 (right). When the Central Railway was laid out in 1899 this pavement was preserved under one of the massive blue brick arches. I remember viewing these Roman remains on site in the 1950s (above).

The mosaic pavement featured above is now on display in the Jewry Wall Museum.

A fine Roman pavement found in St Nicholas Street.

The mosaic on display in the basement of the house of E.A. Goode at 50 St Nicholas Street, 22 April 1911. It was possible to view this mosaic pavement by knocking on the door of the house and paying a few pence. I can clearly remember being conducted into the basement of this property to view these mosaics in the 1950s.

This second-century mosaic of Diana and Acteon was uncovered in a house-building project in the north-east quarter of the town in about 1675. It was considered to be one of the finest examples of a mosaic found in England. When uncovered it was restored and framed in a portable structure to be placed on display, and was one of the first exhibits handed to the town museum. In the second century *Ratae* (Leicester) was developing into a town of considerable importance. This engraving of the mosaic was published in the 1790s and many other drawings of it have been produced. The original is on display in the Jewry Wall Museum. It should be examined carefully to view the Roman artist's attempt to produce a three-dimensional mosaic.

NEW WALK MUSEUM

On New Walk stands the imposing pseudo-classical front to the New Walk Museum. Two huge Russian cannon from the Crimean War stand as sentinels on either side of the main entrance. This fine museum, built in 1837 as a preparatory school, was not a financial success. In 1848 it was purchased by the corporation for £3,300 and they spent a further £1,000 converting the building into the town museum. In 1849 the Literary and Philosophical Society transferred their collection there. They had spent ten years building up a fine collection of artefacts and exhibits for display in such a building.

In 1880 the appointment of Montague Browne as curator brought many changes. A scientist, taxidermist and model-maker of considerable repute, he made sweeping alterations, putting particular emphasis on zoological features. The museum was his life: its display of archaeological remains, local history and the art gallery ensured that it was considered to be one of the finest museums outside London in the Victorian period.

The Town Museum, *c.* 1905. The formal inauguration of this building took place on 19 June 1849 with the presentation of the Literary and Philosophical Society's collection by Colin Macaulay to the Mayor, William Biggs.

Schoolchildren on the New Walk outside the museum, *c.* 1910.

A memorial, by the sculptor Samuel Barfield, that stood on the approach to New Walk Museum was erected in August 1864 in memory of James Francis Hollings. Hollings was Mayor of Leicester from 1859 to 1860 and President of the Literary and Philosophical Society in 1846/7, 1853/4 and 1859/60. The column was erected by his friends. It was demolished in 1955 by the museum's committee who could not agree to the cost of restoration.

Above: A Montague Browne display of herons in 1900.
Left: A 'gentleman' on guard in the museum, 2001.

This is how ornithological exhibits were displayed by Montague Browne in 1900.

Above: Roman remains on display in 1905. Most of these artefacts are now held at Jewry Wall Museum. *Right*: A mummy – a twenty-first century presentation. This museum is an important educational facility well supported by local schools. I have enjoyed a cup of tea in the café and watched children with their teacher working hard in the workrooms available to young and old.

A citiosaurus was discovered in a pit at Great Casterton in Rutland, 19 June 1968. Restored and displayed in the museum, it is one of the finest preserved sauropod dinosaurs in Europe.

A 19 million-year-old plesiosaur on display in the museum, 2001.

New Walk Museum Art Gallery holds a fine collection with many works of art. It also encourages exhibitions which are very well supported by local artists.

A workshop in progress in the museum. Continuous exhibitions and 'hands-on' models and exhibits are made available to teachers and schoolchildren. Professional staff are in attendance to lend their support.

VICTORIA PARK

The park gate entrance to Victoria Park designed by Edwin Lutyens. These two lodges were built between 1931 and 1933. This photograph was taken shortly after the two buildings were erected.

Victoria Park is part of a large area of land granted to the burgesses of Leicester by Simon de Montfort, previously known as Cowhay then South Fields. This area of land was developed into the Leicester racecourse, laid out as the Victoria Park in 1883. Here a mass cricket match is being played by boys on the site of the racecourse in about 1930.

The Lutyens war memorial, erected in 1923. This was a permanent memorial to those from Leicestershire who were killed in the First World War. It replaced the temporary memorial erected in 1917 in Town Hall Square that had inscribed on it names of all those people who died. Why were the inscribed names incorporated on plaques adjacent to this memorial and not re-erected on this site?

The Royal Leicestershire Regiment tiger has now been incorporated on Lutyens's memorial arch. The tiger as a badge was granted by George IV in 1825 and confirmed royal by George VI in 1946.

Around the bandstand on election day, Victoria Park, 1905. The election of a Liberal government is being celebrated.

A pageant entering Victoria Park at the coronation of George V in 1911.

Victoria Park in the 1920s with the pavilion in the background.

The pavilion in Victoria Park, *c.* 1905. It was a fine Victorian building until it was damaged in a bombing raid during the Second World War, after which the remains were demolished. Funding was available, so it could have been rebuilt.

De Montfort Hall in Victoria Park, built in 1913 to a design by Shirley Harrison, and is seen here in a contemporary photograph. The site was given to Leicester by Simon de Montfort.

The interior of De Montfort Hall with a view of the auditorium and the magnificent organ. This photograph was taken in 1913 – the year it was opened.

Above: The bandstand in Victoria Park, 1923, with a group of Leicestershire soldiers playing nostalgic tunes. *Right*: The memorial to the American Airborne troops who trained in Leicestershire prior to the D-Day invasion in the Second World War, erected in Victoria Park.

De Montfort Hall with the city coat of arms displayed above the main entrance, 2001.

5

Into the Future

The National Space Centre dominates the skyline at the Belgrave Lock at the junction of the Grand Union Canal and the River Soar into Abbey Park. An interesting day can be spent walking along the canalside footpath from near Belgrave Gardens, crossing the canal at this weir and using the footbridge close to the lock indicated above. Walk along part of the bank of the River Soar to the National Space Centre and the Abbey Pumping Station. On visiting these two excellent features, spend some time in Abbey Park. By taking a bus trip along Belgrave Road, a pleasant walk is possible. St Margaret's bus station is also only a short walk from the Grand Union Canal. Some historic features can be seen where it leaves Abbey Park at St Margaret's Way.

NATIONAL SPACE CENTRE

Thor Able and Blue Streak rockets were installed in the Rocket Tower at the National Space Centre in October 2000 before it opened in the summer of the following year. A light lunch can be enjoyed and while you eat you can view Thor rising above you!

A senior citizen's ticket to the National Space Centre. This fantastic exhibition was opened to the public on 30 June 2001. It is a most interesting display of scientific discovery, and there are 'hands-on' displays. The multi-media show, 'Big', is worth a visit combined with the 'Great' display itself. Any person, young or old, interested in their world cannot be unimpressed when visiting this marvellous collection. The building was designed by Nicholas Grimshaw and Partners.

A lunar module suspended in the tower.

A Soyuz capsule, restored and 'hanging in space'.

The Columbus module from a space station replica. It is awe-inspiring to consider this structure that floats in space as part of the astronauts' living and working quarters.

An astronaut ready for space.

'The race into space' – one of the first Apollo space capsules to return to earth.

ABBEY PUMPING STATION

Abbey Pumping Station opened in 1891 and closed in 1964. It was preserved because of the four magnificent beam steam engines. These large pumps were built to pump Leicester's sewage from the town to the sewage treatment works at Beaumont Leys. The engines were built by Gimsons of Leicester and are rare working Woolf compound beam engines.

Above: Examples of Roman and medieval sewage pipes, found in Leicester. *Left*: An Edwardian cast-iron *pissoir* standing outside the Pumping Station Museum.

Above: One of the beam engines. On certain days during special steam events these engines can be seen working. *Left*: A preserved section of one of the brick-built sewers that were constructed under the streets of Leicester.

THE GRAND UNION

Locks at Frog Island between Northgate and Woodgate on the A50. This area of Leicester is steeped in history. A walk along the Grand Union Canal is a must for all those interested in the industrial development of this city. Spend some time on the walk visiting the local pubs. To the left of the locks above stands the North Bridge Tavern, an industrial pub well worth a visit for refreshment on an active walk.

This is a marvellous location on a walk along the Grand Union Canal/River Soar. Belgrave Locks are on the left, with the weir controlling the River Soar on the right. Standing high in the background is the National Space Centre.

A few yards along the Grand Union Canal from Belgrave Locks is Swan Nest Footbridge, built across the canal in 1975.

Barges moored at the Waterside Centre on the River Soar are connected to the canal through the locks at Belgrave where the height of the river is controlled by weirs. Again the Space Centre dominates the background.

A stretch of the Grand Union Canal as it passes through the city. There are warehouses on the left and the towpath is on the right. In 1778 the first length of canal in Leicestershire was opened with the canalisation of the River Soar for 9 miles from the River Trent to Loughborough. Considerable negotiations were needed before the canal was extended into Leicester. It was officially opened on 24 October 1794.

A narrowboat used as a houseboat passes under the St Margaret's Way bridge off Abbey Park. The footpath is on the right.

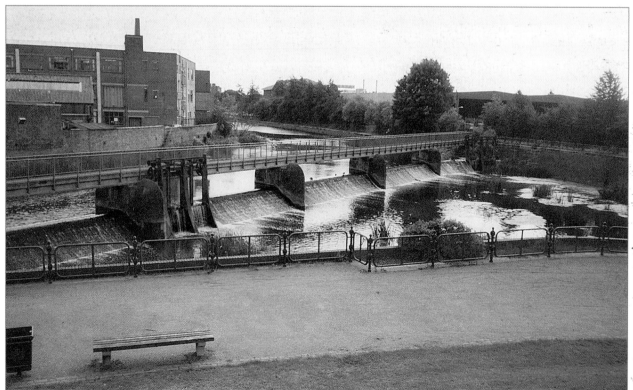

Evans Weir is a most interesting feature of the Grand Union Canal and the River Soar. At this point the navigation is higher than the river and a footbridge stands across the top of the weir off Soar Lane at Black Friars.

Soar Point public house on the Grand Union Canal at the Newarke Street Bridge – a haven for De Montfort University students, 2001.

A narrowboat passes under the Newarke Street Bridge, seen from the terrace of the Soar Point pub on the canal bank, 2001.

Don taking refreshments in the front of the Quay public house at Bede Island, on the Western Boulevard along the side of the Grand Union Canal, 2001.

The remains of the Great Central Railway near the canal at West Bridge, 2001. Will this Victorian bridge be retained for posterity?

A narrowboat about to negotiate its way under Upperton Road bridge, 2001.

Oxford Street Antiques

Many people would miss this warehouse that is situated virtually opposite the Magazine Gateway, via the underpass leading on to Oxford Street. If you have time to kill and an interest in antiques, it is worth visiting this excellent display. If nothing else, it is an historic collection well worth viewing.

A display of antiques in 2001.

Paintings and prints on display in one of the stairways to various parts of the warehouse.

Keith examining some of the prints on display in one of the many collections.

A display of furniture laid out in the entrance foyer to the antiques centre, 2001.

JAIN CENTRE

The Jain Centre on Oxford Street, 2001 – the 2,600th birthday of Bhagwan Mahavir and the birth of the Jain faith.

Above: An exterior view of the Jain Centre on Oxford Street. It was constructed from a deconsecrated Methodist church. *Left*: It is a magnificent temple, and this is a photograph of one of the exterior carvings. This building is well worth a visit just to view the excellent carvings inside.

St Martin's Square

St Martin's Square, situated close to Leicester Cathedral, bordered by Loseby Lane, Cank Street, Silver Street and St Martin's Walk.

St Martin's Walk leading on to St Martin's Square, from Cank Street.

Keith and me enjoying an excellent Italian meal in the Altoco restaurant in St Martin's Square, 2001.

HOTELS

The Belmont House Hotel is on the New Walk, very close to the New Walk Museum.

The Holiday Inn is opposite the Jewry Wall Museum; both were built on the site of Roman Leicester. On the following page are two more city hotels that are situated within easy walking distance of all the attractions featured in this book. There are many other hotels in the city. Should you wish to stay in the city as a visitor, contact the local tourist office, situated on Every Street.

The Goose on Hotel Street, standing virtually opposite one of the many entrances to the famous Market Place. It is an historic name that applies to this area of the city, principally because of the Royal Hotel on Horsefair Street and the Saracen's Head were off the Market Place.

The Grand Hotel on Granby Street, 2001.

TOURISTS

Leicester Tourist Centre on Every Street, opposite the Town Hall, 2001.

If you want to know the best way to see the sights in Leicester, contact the tourist centre. It is staffed by very helpful people and has a fine display of local history books on show and for sale – particularly those produced by Sutton Publishing.

The tourist office can make arrangements for visitors to stay in Leicester and in other locations around the UK.

BIBLIOGRAPHY

Armitage, D.M.E., *Heraldry in Leicestershire Churches* (vol. 1), 1990
Bailey, Brian J., *Portrait of Leicestershire*, 1977
Beresiner, Yasha, *British County Maps*, 1983
Bown, Mark, *Leicester Trams*, 1995
Britton, John, *County of Leicester*, 1815
Bryant, Sir Arthur, *1,000 years of the British Monarchy*, 1973
Cavanagh, Terry, *Public Sculpture of Leicestershire and Rutland*, 2000
Featherstone, Thomas, *Legends of Leicester*, 1838
Fielding-Johnson, Agnes, *Glimpses of Ancient Leicester*, 1906
Flower, John, *Views of the Ancient Buildings in the Town and County of Leicester*, 1826
Fox, Levi, *Leicester Castle*, 1944
Hoskins, W.G., *A Shell Guide, Leicestershire*, 1970
Inglis, G.S. (ed.), *The Arms of the City of Leicester*, 1932
McWhirr, Alan (ed.), *Sycamore Leaves*, 1985
Nichols, John, *The History and Antiquities of the County of Leicester* (4 vols in 8), 1795–1811
North, Thomas, *Churchwardens of St Martin's*, 1884
Ogilby, John, *Britannia*, 1675
Palmer, Roy, *The Folklore of Leicestershire and Rutland*, 1985
Pevsner, Nikolaus, *Leicestershire & Rutland*, 1984 edn
Read, Robert jnr, *Modern Leicester*, 1881
Russell, Percy, *A Leicestershire Road*, 1934
Skillington, Florence, *The Plain Man's History of Leicester*, 1950
Smiegielski, W.K., *Leicester Today and Tomorrow*, 1968
Speed, John, *History of Britain*, 1611
Spencer's Almanack, 1899, 1900, 1901
Stevenson, Joan, *Leicester Through the Ages*, 1995
Throsby, John, *The Ancient Town of Leicester*, 1791
Transactions of the Leicestershire Archaeological Society (vols 1–20), 1855–1939

The boathouse, Abbey Park on the River Soar, *c.* 1910.

ACKNOWLEDGEMENTS

Since the late 1930s I have been interested in the city of Leicester, after visiting the Abbey Park Show with my mother and father and their friends just before the start of the Second World War. I have casually retained information and discussed the city with many of my friends, and it is through the information that has been provided over the last fifty years that the production of this book has been possible. Particular thanks must be expressed to Don Humberston, Jo Humberston, David Humberston, Mark Bown, John Lucas of the Jewry Wall Museum and Joan North, the vice-president of the Leicestershire Archaeological and Historical Society. Many of the photographs and illustrations printed in this book are out of copyright; where the copyright is retained it is held by myself. Once again I must thank Pat Peters for processing the manuscript and Sutton Publishing for accepting this compilation for publication.

Rugby, cricket and football are all played in the city of Leicester.

Selective Index